165 Super Bad Jokes for Teachers

Jokes to make you groan, smile, and roll your eyes!

Dedication/Apology

Introducing "101 Super Bad Jokes for Teachers" – a humorous tribute to the remarkable educators who tirelessly inspire and enlighten generations of learners. This book is dedicated to all the teachers who infuse knowledge with laughter and create unforgettable classroom experiences.

Inside these pages, you'll discover a collection of jokes that will bring a smile to your face and elicit groans and laughter. From witty puns to clever one-liners, these jokes offer a delightful break from the daily rigors of teaching. However, a word of caution: share them in moderation, as repeated use may lead to questioning glances from friends, colleagues, and students.

I would also like to thank (and apologize to) my family for putting up with me all these years. Your patience in listening to my dribble has been instrumental in my determination to come up with these ever more clever and horrendous jokes that I am now sharing with you all.

Finally, to my boat family and friends - thank you for everything!

You guys are the best!

Why did the math book look sad?

Because it had too many problems!

Why did the teacher wear sunglasses to school?

Because her students were so bright!

Why don't scientists trust atoms?

Because they make up everything!

Why did the scarecrow become a teacher?

Because he was outstanding in his field!

How do you make a tissue dance?

You put a little boogie in it!

Why did the teacher bring a ladder to class?

To help the students reach for the stars!

What did one pencil say to the other pencil?

"You're looking sharp!"

Why did the teacher wear a life jacket in the classroom?

Because the students were making waves!

Why did the music teacher need a ladder?

To reach the high notes!

How do you fix a broken pizza?

With tomato paste!

What's the best time to go to the dentist?

Tooth-hurty!

Why was the math book sad?

It had too many problems!

How did the geography teacher explore the world?

She took a globe-trotting vacation!

Why did the student bring a ladder to school?

To reach the highest grades!

Why don't plants like math?

Because they don't like square roots!

What do you call a dinosaur that's a great teacher?

A dino-scholar!

Why did the student eat their homework?

Because the teacher said it was a piece of cake!

Why was the computer cold?

It left its Windows open!

What did the math teacher say when she got a new student?

*"Welcome!
I hope you'll find
this place quite
sum-thing!"*

What did one pencil say to the other pencil at school?

"You're looking sharp today!"

Why did the teacher bring a ladder to the classroom?

To help the students reach for the stars!

Why did the clock in the school always get good grades?

It knew how to tick all the right boxes!

What do you call a bear without any books?

Barely educated!

Why did the student bring a ladder to the library?

Because they heard it had high shelves!

What do you call a teacher who never smiles?

A ruler!

Why did the teacher wear sunglasses during class?

Because her students were so bright, she needed to shade her eyes!

What did the pencil say to the paper?

"I dot my i's on you!"

Why did the math teacher open a bakery?

Because she kneaded a change of π!

What's a teacher's favorite type of music?

Class-ical!

Why did the teacher go to the beach?

To test the waters!

How do you make an apple turnover?

Push it down a hill!

Why did the teacher take the class to space?

To change the classroom atmosphere!

What's a teacher's favorite type of footwear?

Well-heeled shoes!

Why did the teacher always have a ladder in their classroom?

To help their students reach for their dreams!

Why did the teacher bring a broom to school?

To sweep the students off their feet with knowledge!

What do you call a teacher who can sing?

A pitch-perfect educator!

Why did the teacher write on the window?

Because they wanted their lesson to be crystal clear!

Why was the math book so unhappy?

Because it didn't have enough solutions!

Why did the teacher always carry a pencil and paper?

To draw their students' attention!

What do you call a teacher who never frowns?

A pro-fessor!

Why did the teacher bring a ladder to the art room?

To reach the highest levels of creativity!

Why should you never call someone "average"?

It's just mean!

What's a teacher's favorite type of dessert?

Pi!

How do you organize an outer space party for your students?

You just planet!

Why was the science book so good at basketball?

It had all the chemical reactions!

What do you call a teacher who loves to garden?

A plant-educator!

Why did the teacher bring a shovel to class?

To dig deep into the subject matter!

Why did the English teacher always have a ladder?

To reach the highest literature!

Why was the math book worried it's keys?

It was concerned it did not have the right answers!

Why did the music teacher always carry a ladder?

To reach the high notes!

Why did the teacher use a ladder during art class?

To draw their students' attention!

How do you make a lemon drop?

Just let it fall during chemistry class!

What do you call a teacher who never loses their voice?

A vocal-chord master!

Why did the teacher bring a ladder to the gym?

To help students climb to new heights!

What did the science teacher say to the struggling student?

"You'll get a reaction out of me!"

What did the teacher who was scared of elevators do?

They took steps to avoid them.

Why was the chemistry teacher great at solving problems?

They had all the right elements!

What's a teacher's favorite type of exercise?

Gymnastics—because they love to stretch their students' minds!

Why did the teacher always carry a map?

To stay on course with their lessons!

What did the teacher say to the misbehaving pencil?

"You need to lead by example!"

Why did the teacher bring a ruler to the park?

To measure how long the students played!

Why did the teacher bring a parachute to school?

To help their students land softly on the path to success!

What's a teacher's favorite type of coffee?

Teach-aroma!

Why did the teacher bring a camera to school?

To capture all the priceless moments of learning!

What do you call a teacher with superpowers?

A "lesson"ed superhero!

Why was six afraid of seven?

Because seven, eight, nine!

Why did the teacher always carry a telescope?

To keep an eye on all the bright stars in the classroom!

Why did the teacher bring a ladder to the library?

To reach the highest shelves of knowledge!

Why did the teacher go to the bank?

To learn about the currency of knowledge!

What did the teacher say to the celery?

"You can't beet knowledge!"

Why did the teacher bring a ladder to the assembly?

To raise the students' spirits!

What's a teacher's
favorite kind of plant?

A "mul-teacher" plant!

Why did the teacher bring a ladder to the art museum?

To get a better perspective on the masterpieces!

Why did the teacher bring a ladder to the concert?

To help the students reach new heights of musical talent!

What did the pencil sharpener say to the pencil?

Stop going in circles and get to the point.

Which dinosaur has the best vocabulary?

Thesaurus-Rex.

Teacher: "Name two pronouns?"

Student: "Who, me?"

Why did the kids cross the playground?

To get to the other slide!

What pencil did Shakespeare write with?

2B

How do bees get to school?

They ride the school buzz!

What is smarter than a talking dog?

A Spelling Bee!

I'm close friends with 25 letters of the alphabet...

I don't know Y

Why did the scarecrow win a Nobel Prize?

For being "out standing" in his field

What is a teacher's favorite candy?

Smarties!

Why is a piano so hard to open?

Because the keys are on the inside!

What do you call a belt made from watches?

A waist of time

I have never met a three...

...but I have a metaphor!

What did the ghost teacher say to the class?

"Look at the board and I will go through it again."

If April flowers bring May flowers, what do Mayflowers bring?

Pilgrims!

How many eggs do French folk have for breakfast?

One. Because one egg is un œuf

Did you know old math teachers never die?

They just lose some of their functions!

Which school teachers have the greenest thumbs?

The kinder-garden teachers!

Why were the early days of history called the dark ages?

Because there were so many knights!

Where was the Declaration of Independence signed?

At the bottom!

What do you call bears with no ears?

B

What do you say to comfort a Grammar teacher?

There Their They're

What do you call an acid with an attitude?

A-Mean-Oh-Acid!

Why are witches good at writing?

They are good spellers!

What do you call Santa's brothers and sisters?

Relative clauses

Double negatives...

...are a big NO-NO

Student: "Can I go to the toilet?"

Teacher: "I don't know, can you?"

There's a fine line between a numerator and a denominator.

Unfortunately, only a fraction of you will get this.

Went to the Fibonacci conference last week...

and it was as good as the last two put together

What do you call a teacher who forgot to take attendance?

Absent-minded

Who's the king of the classroom?

The ruler!

Teacher: "What is the most common phrase used in school?"

Student: "I don't know!"
Teacher: "Correct!"

Never date an apostrophe.

They're too possessive

One tectonic plate bumped into another one and said:

"Oops, my fault!"

What is a teacher's favorite nation?

Expla-nation!

Why did the teacher jump into the ocean?

To test the waters!

What's your favorite element?

Helium. I can't speak highly enough about it!

What do you call a music teacher with problems?

A trebled man!

Why was the geometry class always tired?

Because they were all out of shape

Since light travels faster than sound...

...people may appear smart until you hear them speak

Be like a proton...

Always positive!

Child: "I think we need a new teacher."

Mom: "Why's that?"

Child: "Our teacher doesn't know anything! She keeps asking us for the answers..."

There are 10 types of people that understand binary.

Those that do and those that don't

You can throw an envelope as far as you want...

but it'll still be stationary.

Teacher: "What did they do at the do at the Boston Tea Party?"

Student: "I don't know, I wasn't invited!"

Student: "I don't think I deserved zero on this test!"

Teacher: "I agree, but that's the lowest mark I could give you."

What do you call a Frenchman in sandals?

Philippe Philoppe

What's the difference between a cat and a comma?

One has claws at the end of its paws

The other is a pause at the end of a clause

What is a math teacher's favorite dessert?

Pumpkin-Pi!

Why was the fraction sceptical about marrying the decimal?

Because he would have to convert

Why didn't the banana go to school?

It wasn't peeling well!

What is a snake's favorite subject in school?

Hisss-tory!

What did the math team call themselves?

The AlgeBROS

A neutron walks into a bar, and asks the bartender for a drink.

The bartender responds: "For you, no charge."

Is it better to be hot or cold when playing tag during recess?

Hot because you can always catch a cold!

I've been working on a Scandinavian joke.

But it's not quite Finnish

Why does Sweden have barcodes on all of its ships?

So when they return to port - they can Scan-di-navy-in.

I like Geography...

You really know where you are with Geography

Did you hear about the kidnapping at school?

It's OK, he woke up!

Why doesn't the sun have to go to school?

It's bright enough!

What kind of doctor is Dr. Pepper?

A Fizzz-ician!

What did Mason say to Dixon?

We've got to draw the line here!

How was the Roman Empire cut in half?

With a pair of Caesars!

Why do bees have sticky hair?

Because they have honeycombs!

Do fish go on vacation?

No, because they're always in schools!

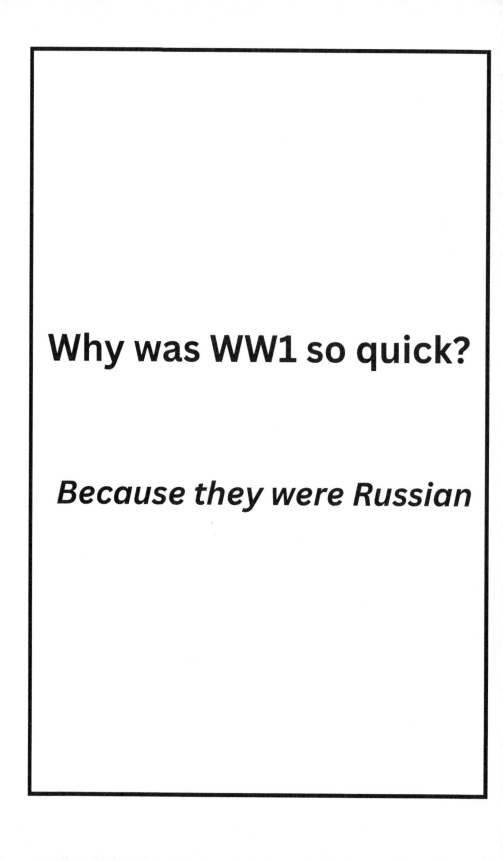

Why was WW1 so quick?

Because they were Russian

What did the buffalo say to his son when he left for college?

Bison!

Last night I dreamt I wrote "The Lord of the Rings".

Then I realized I was just Tolkien in my sleep

Why can't basketball players go on vacation?

They would get called for traveling!

When do you go on red and stop at green?

When you're eating a watermelon!

Why did the librarian get kicked off the plane?

Because it was overbooked!

Why is a baseball game a good place to go on a hot day?

Because there are lots of fans!

Teacher: Why can't freshwater fish live in salt water?

Student: The salt would give them high blood pressure

What does a Math Teacher climb for fun?

Geome-tree!

What is a pirate's favorite subject?

Arrrrrrt!

Why did the little girl like vegetables so much?

She was a Kinder-gardener!

Teacher: If I had 8 oranges in one hand and 10 apples in the other hand, what would I have?

Student: Big hands!

Why were the teacher's eyes crossed?

Because she could not control her pupils!

Teacher: You missed school yesterday, didn't you?

Student: Not really

What do you do if a teacher rolls her eyes at you?

Pick them up and roll them back!

Teacher: What is the shortest month?

Student: May, it only has three letters

How is an English teacher like a judge?

They both give out sentences!

Teacher: If you got $20 from 5 people, what do you get?

Student: A new bike!

What do you call an English teacher with a social media addiction?

Instagrammar

On the first day of school, what did the teacher say were her three favorite words?

June, July, and August

Why was WW2 so slow?

Because they were Stalin

Teacher: "Make a sentence with the words 'defense, detail, and defeat'."

Student: "When a horse jumps over the fence, the feet go before the tail."

"What is the definition of a lecturer?"

Student: "Someone with the bad habit of talking while other people are sleeping!"

Student: "Teacher, you wouldn't punish me for something I didn't do, right?"

Teacher: "Of course not."

Student: "Good! Because I didn't do my homework."

Teacher: "I may always tell you to follow your dreams...

...*but that doesn't mean I'll let you sleep in class!*

Student: Sorry I'm late to class, there was sign down the road...

Teacher: What does the sign have to do with you being late?

Student: The sign said, "School Ahead, Go Slow!"

Printed in Great Britain
by Amazon

42847903R00096